AF263971

The tears of the world are a constant quantity. For each one who begins to weep somewhere else another stops. The same is true of the laugh.

—Samuel Beckett, *Waiting for Godot*

There are tears at the heart of things.

—Virgil, *The Aeneid*
(translated by Seamus Heaney)

Buckman Publishing LLC
est. 2018
1448 NE 28th Ave
Portland, Oregon 97232
buckmanjournal.com

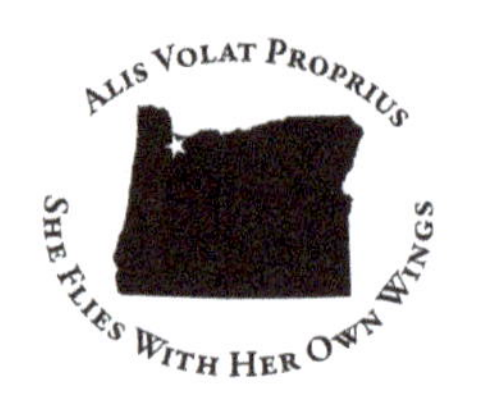

Congratulations! A Buckman production is in your hands! We're an unorthodox operation that continues the daredevil tradition of literature, printing new sparks that ignite imagination. Proudly independent, Buckman's defiant attitude aims to inspire and increase readership in greater society.

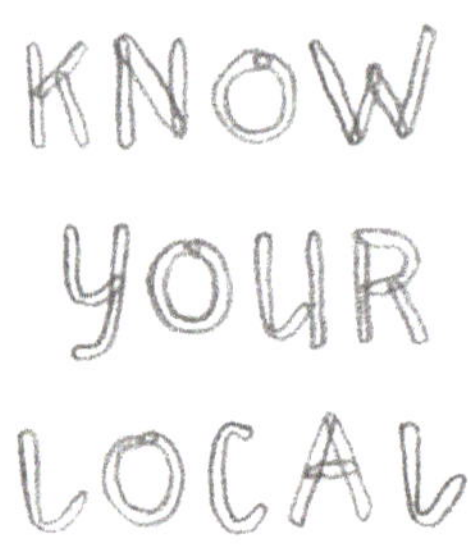

Buckman operates from our home in the upper left of Turtle Island at the confluence of the Whilamut and Wimahl rivers, waters and lands stewarded by the Cayuse, Clackamas, Multnomah, St'pulmsh (Cowlitz) Umatilla, Walla Walla, and Watlala peoples.

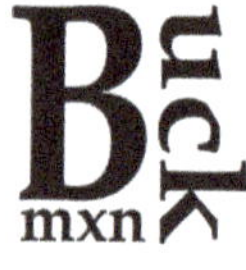

Artwork & Words © 2026
Kira Lynn Cain
Design & Hand Lettering:
Ellen Robinette
Typefaces: Garamond Premier Pro,
NOODLE FONT

ISBN: 9781967058075

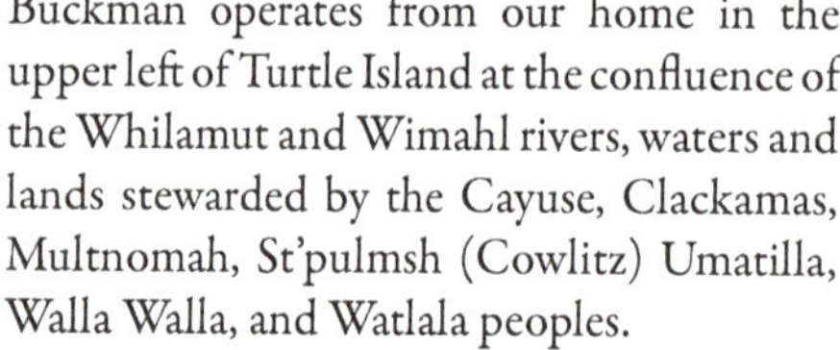

Tears Are Everywhere

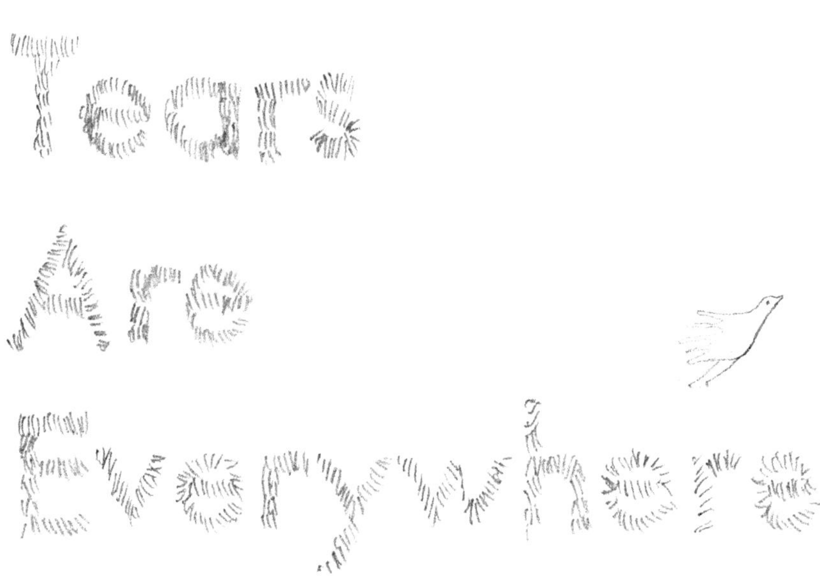

KIRA LYNN CAIN

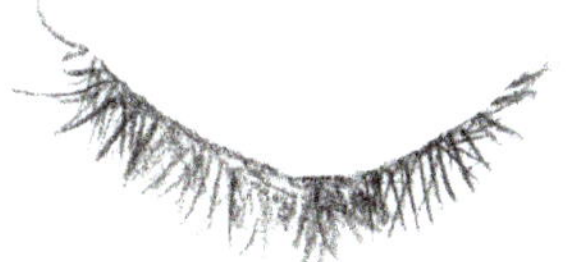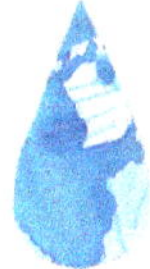

LOOK.

TEARS ARE EVERYWHERE.

YOU SEE THEM

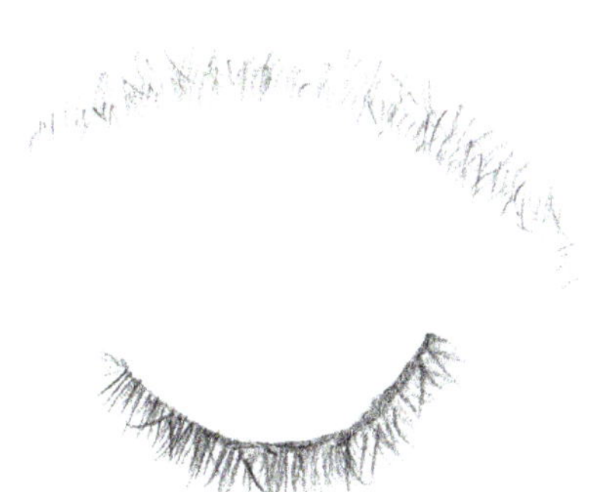
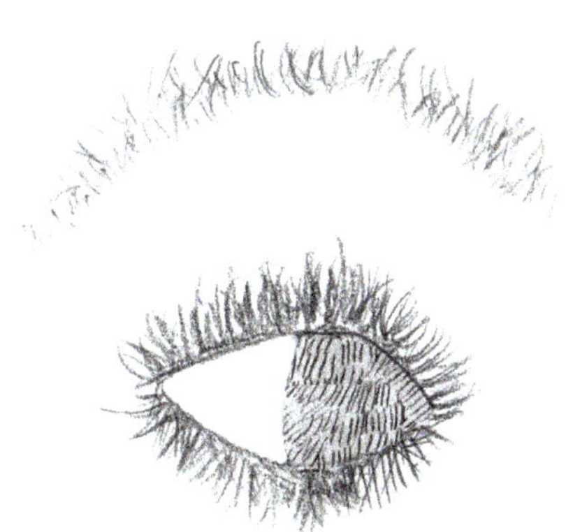
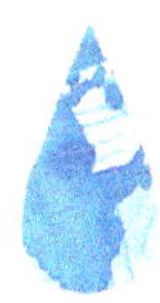

SECRETLY.

TEARS IN THE SEA.

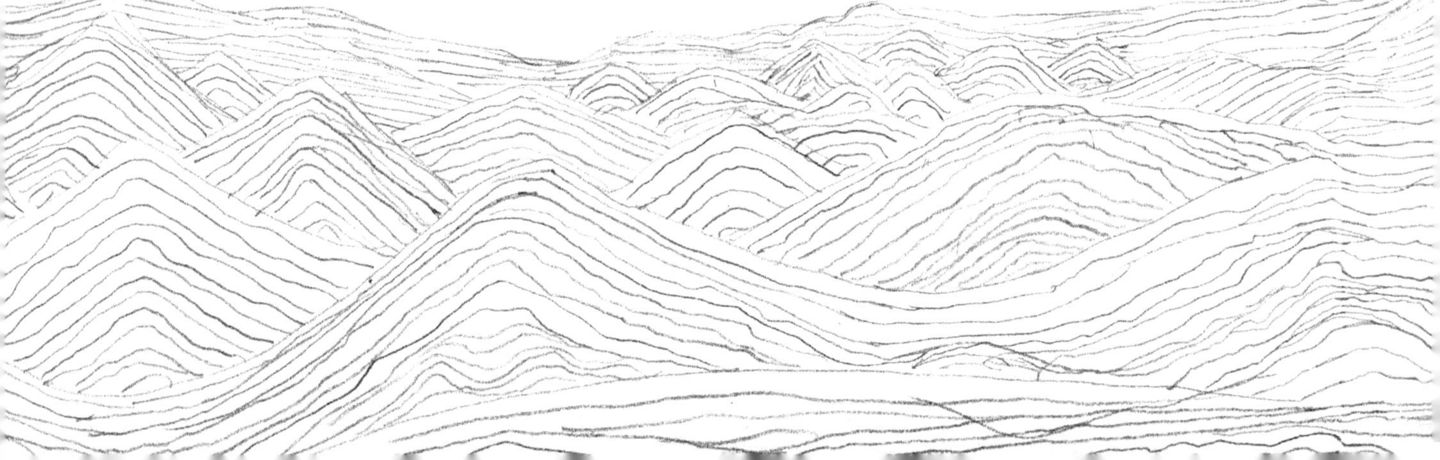

SLOWLY UP,

SILENT DOWN.

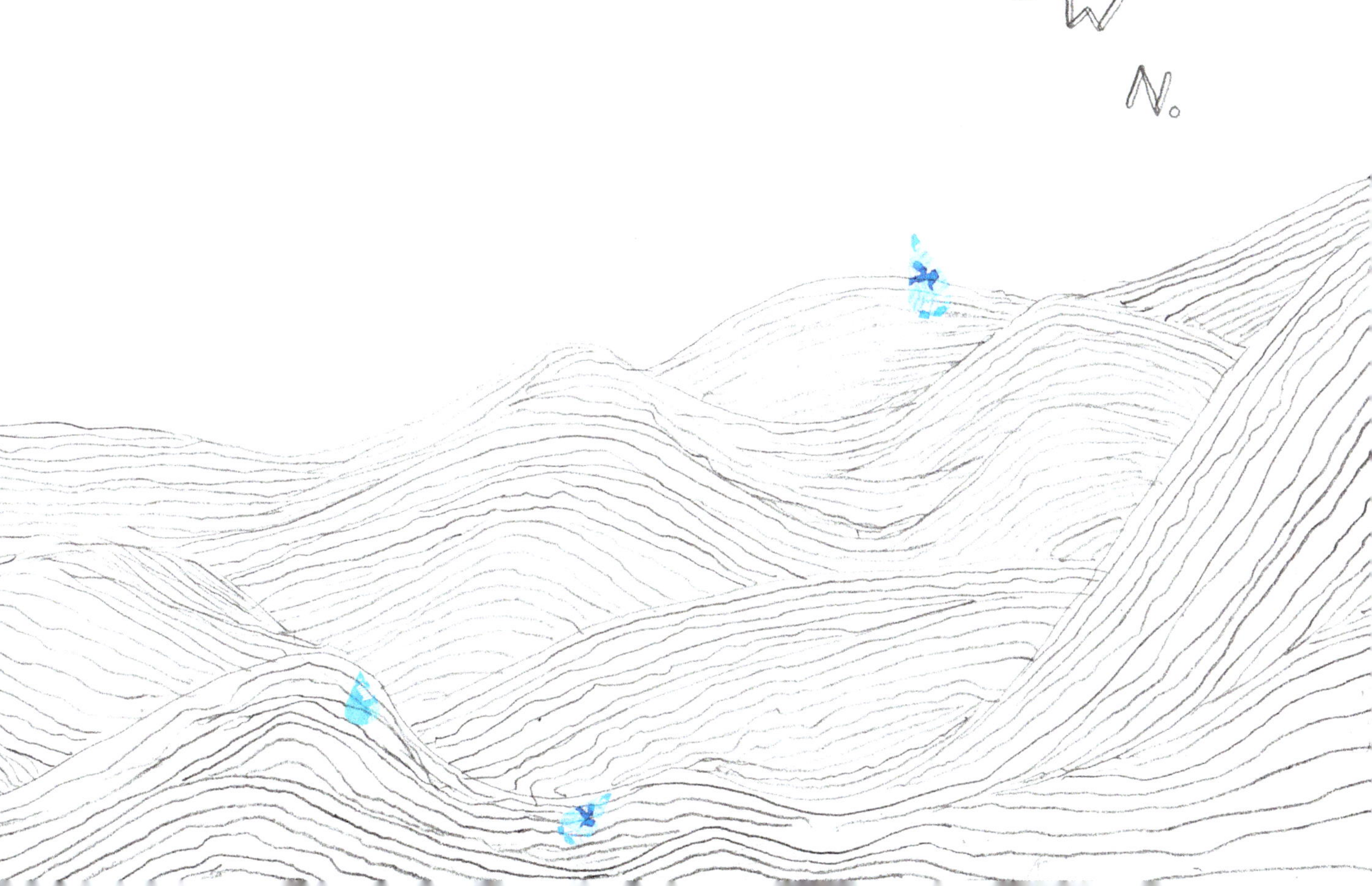

TEARS

IN

THE

SKY,

ASLEEP, ASLEEP.

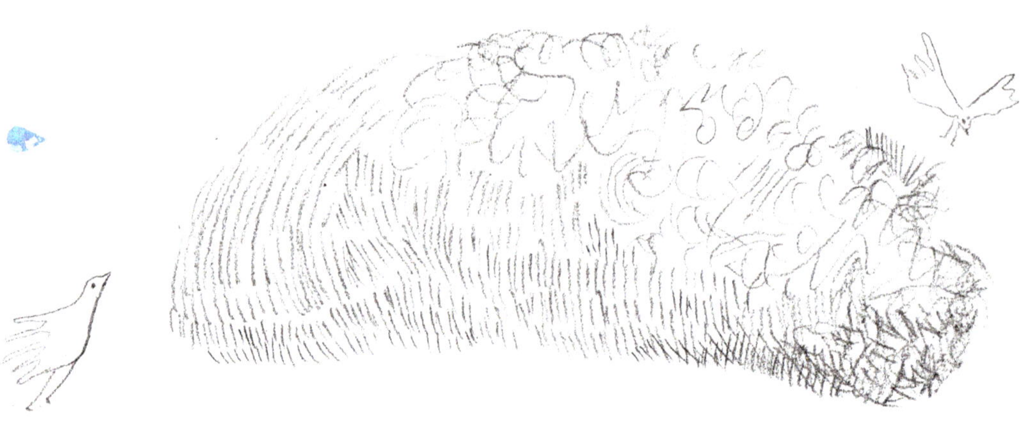

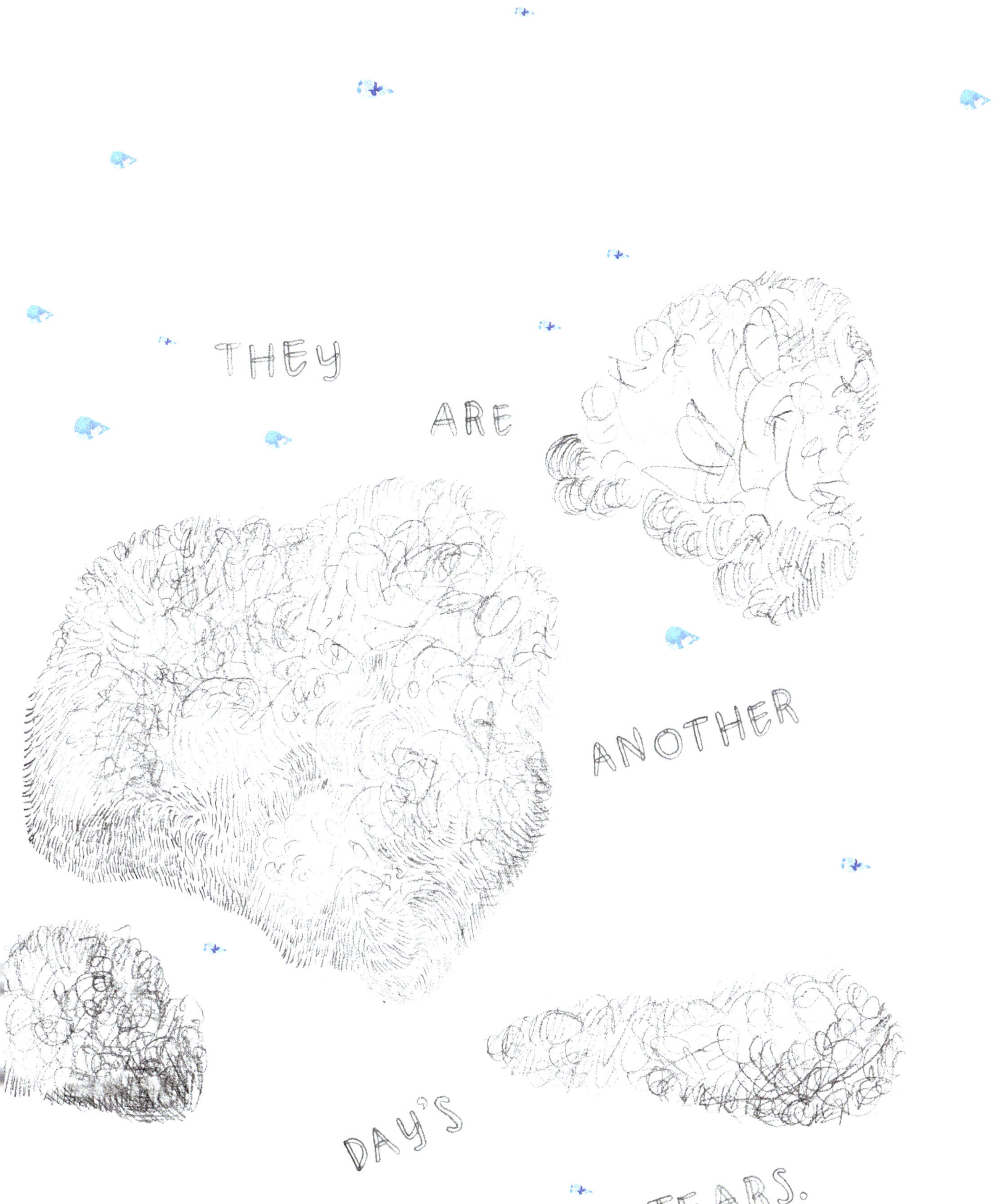

THEY ARE

ANOTHER

DAY'S

TEARS.

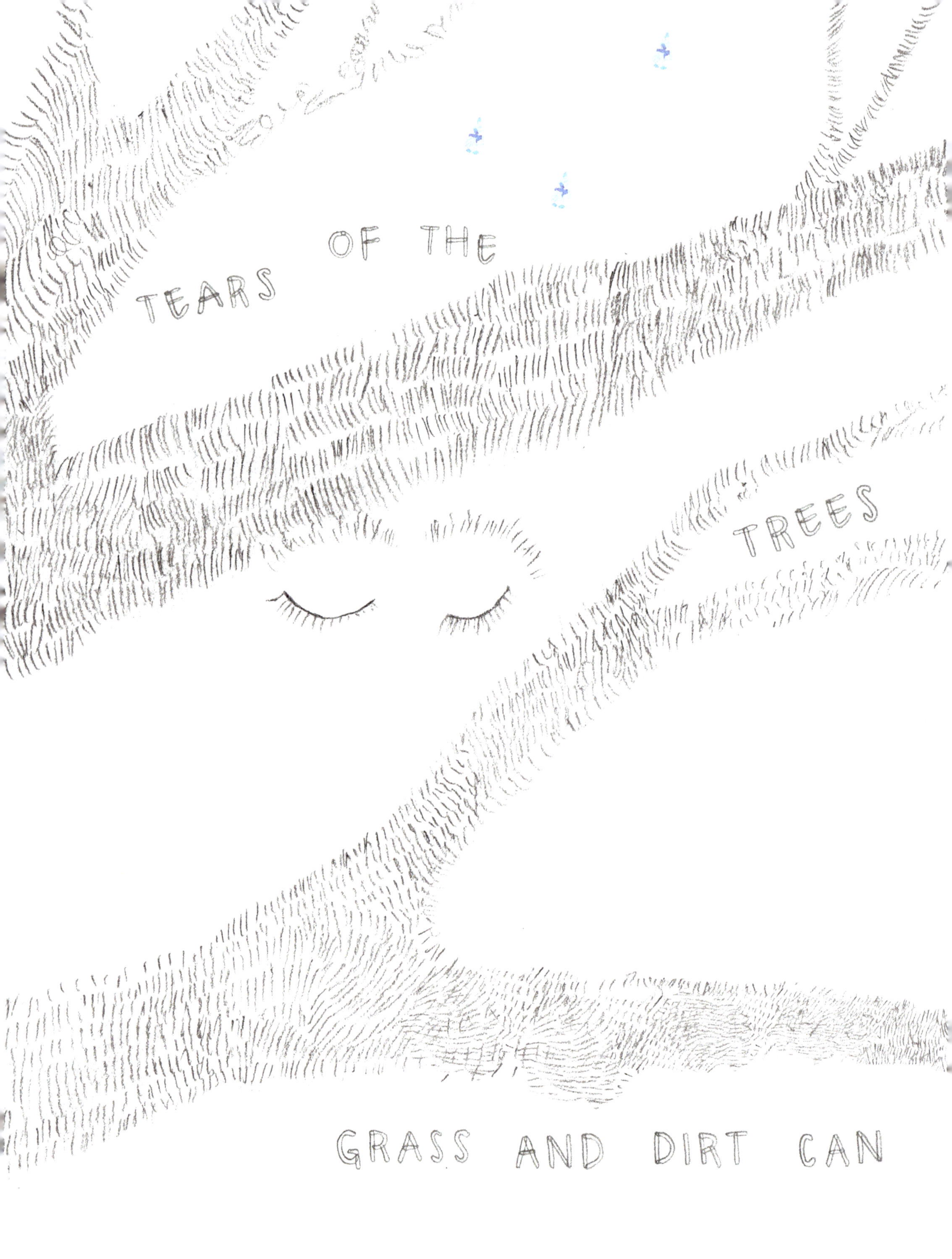

TEARS OF THE
TREES
GRASS AND DIRT CAN

ABOVE.

DRINK THEM.

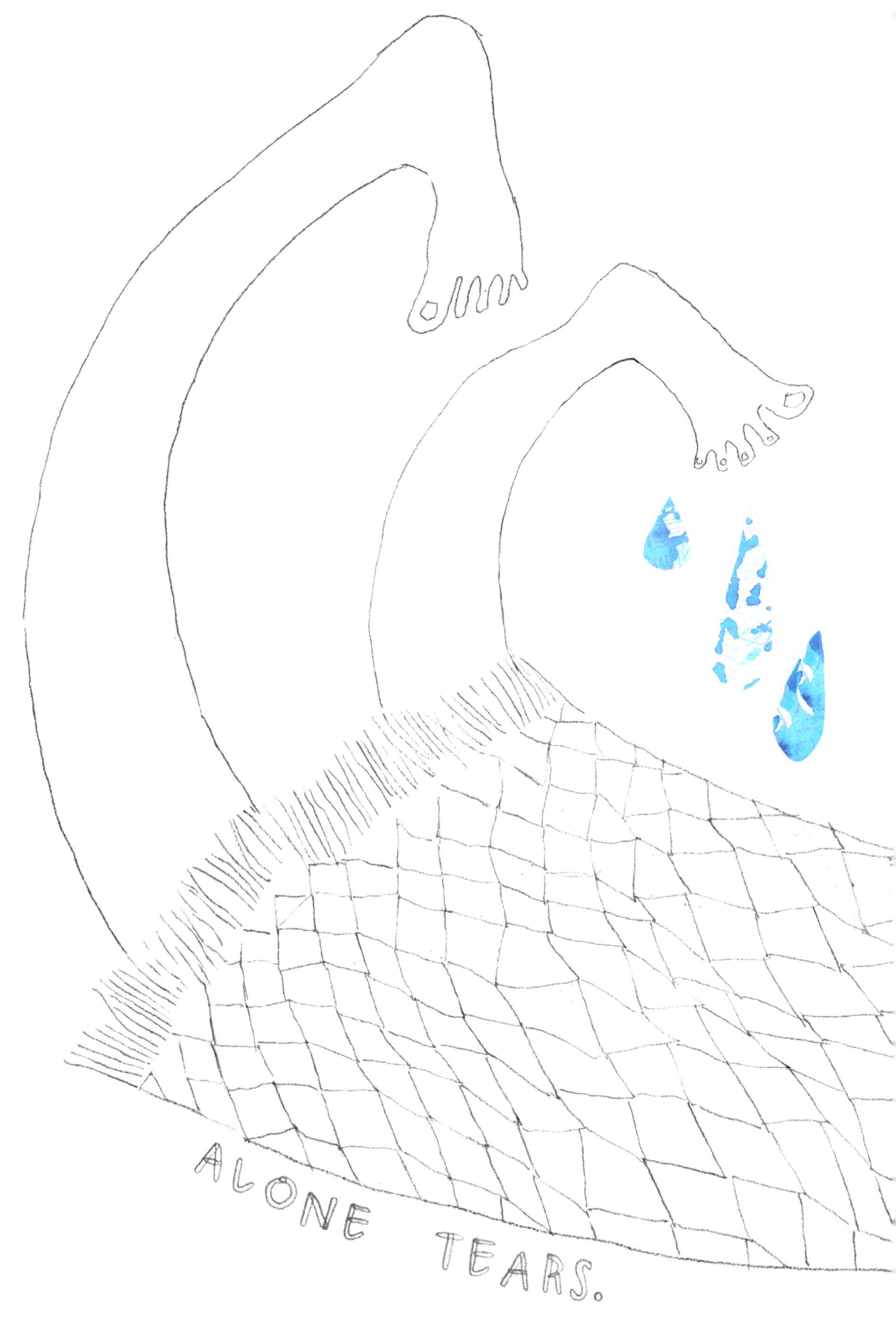
ALONE TEARS.

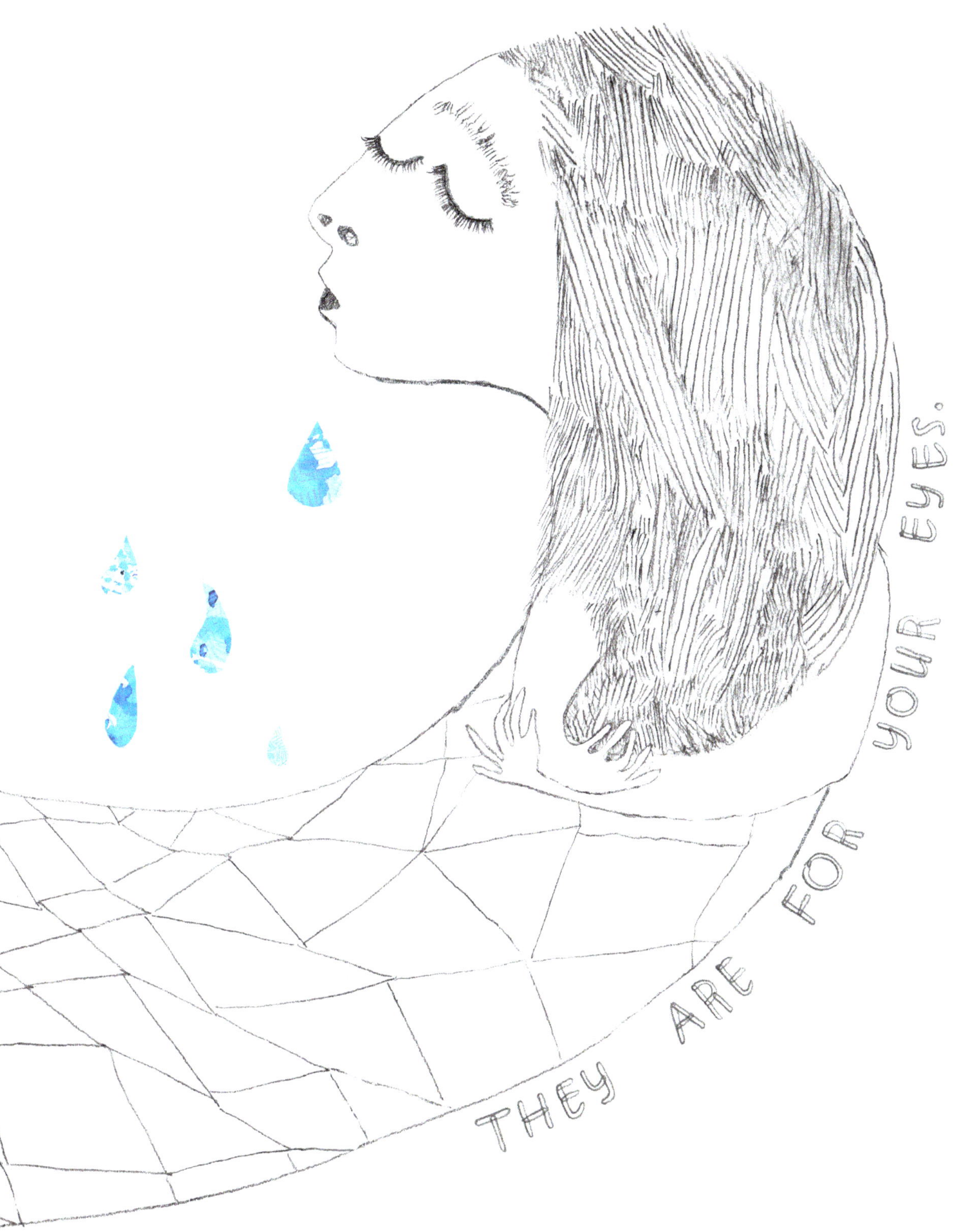

THEY ARE FOR YOUR EYES.

THEY
POOL FORWARD TOWARDS
FLOWERS.

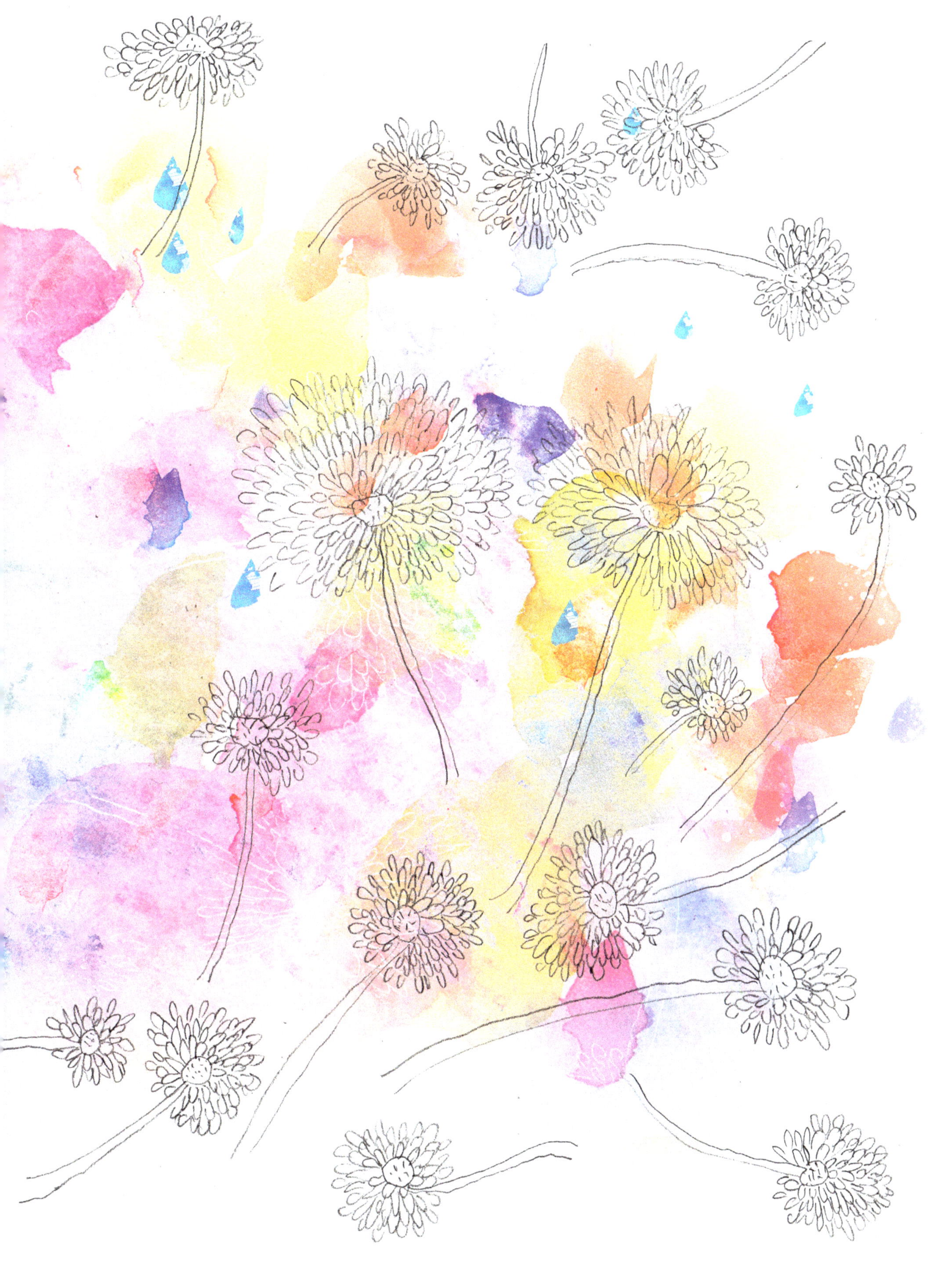

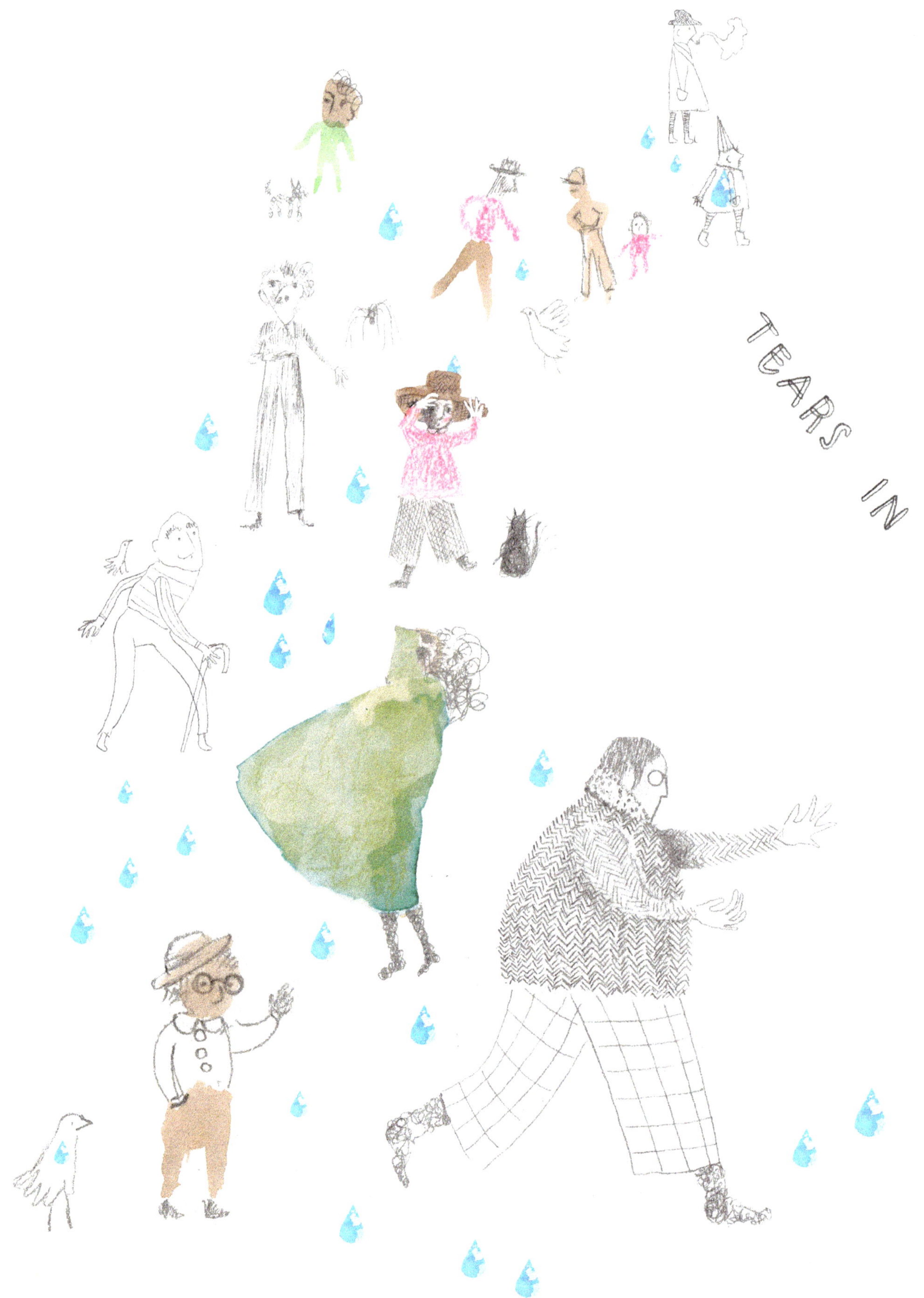
TEARS IN

A CROWD. CLOCKWORK.

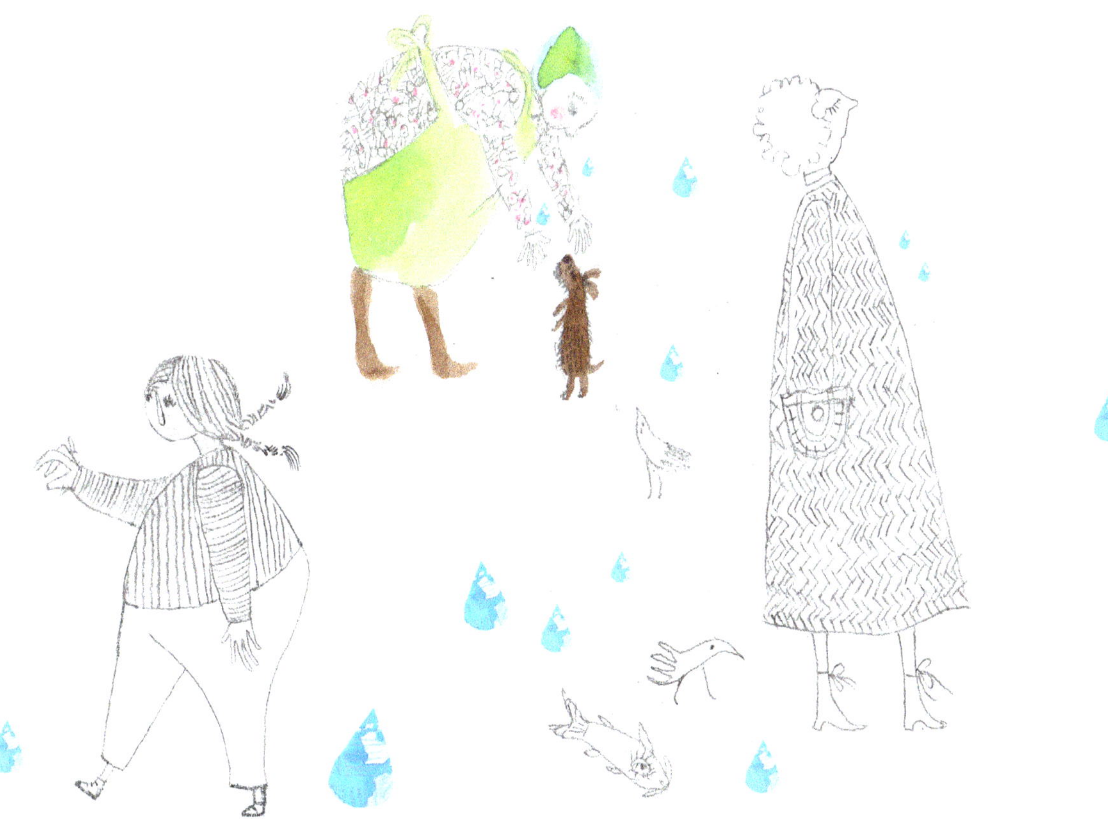

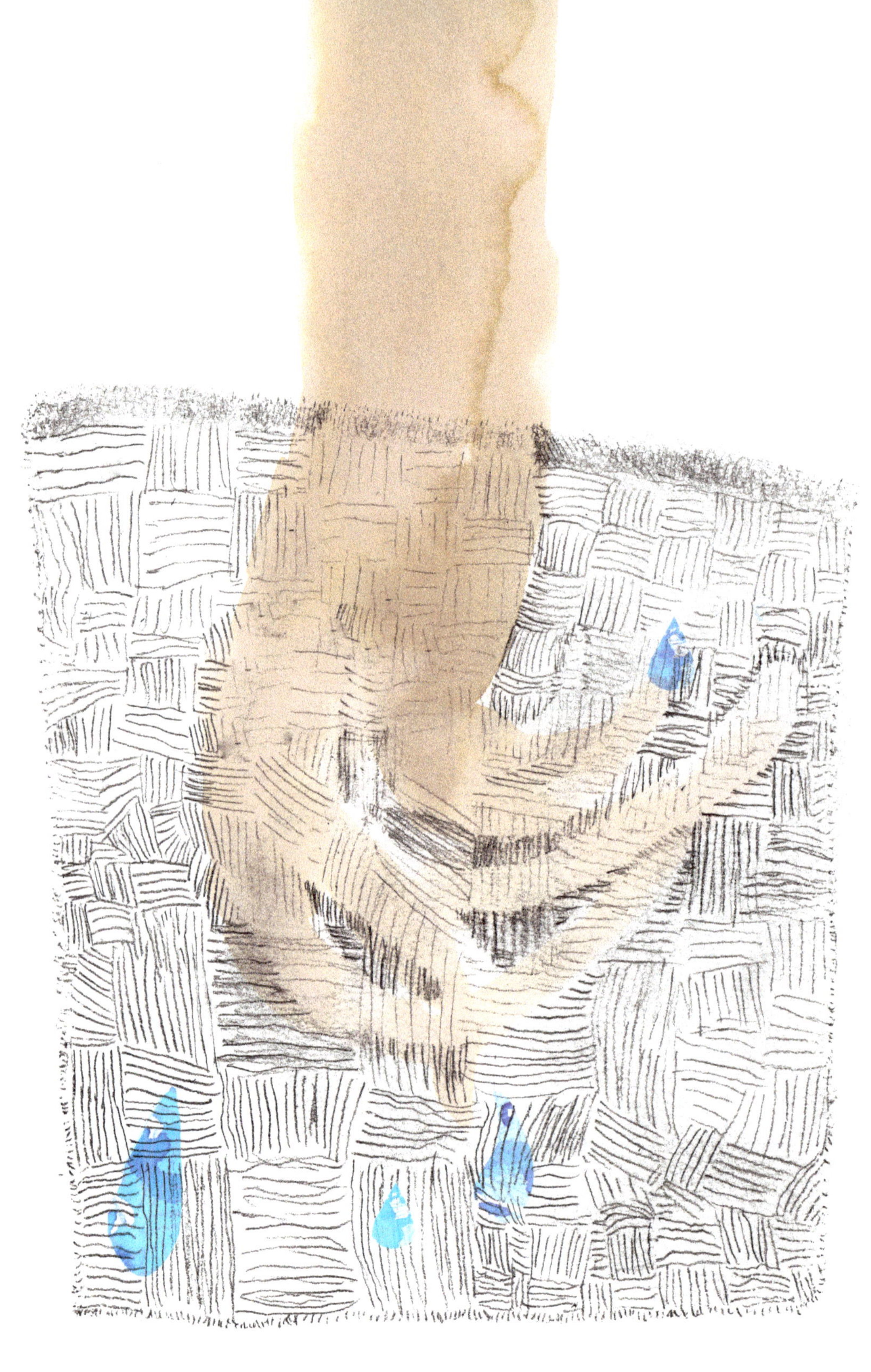

TEARS IN POCKETS.

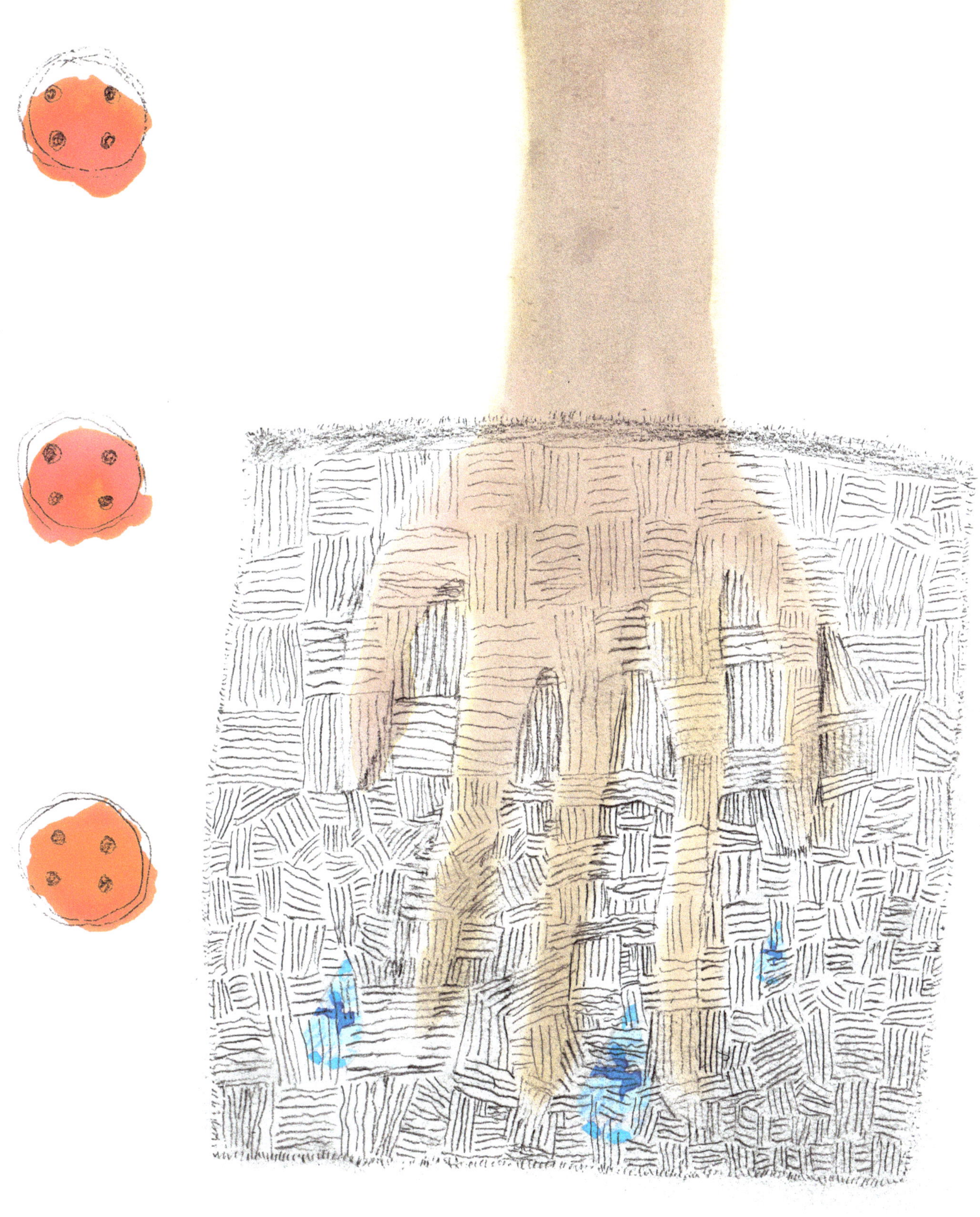

TEARS ON HANDS.

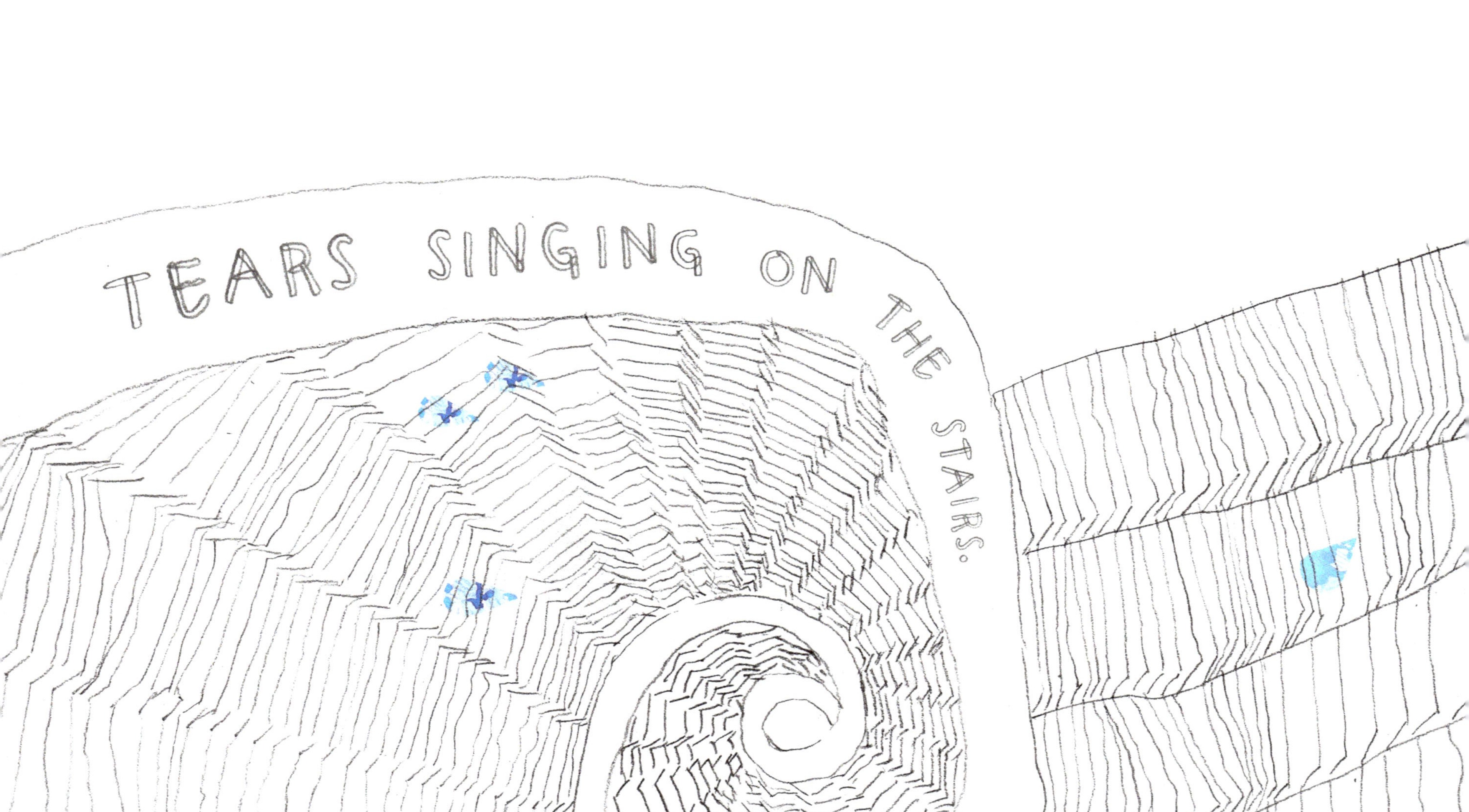

TEARS SINGING ON THE STAIRS.

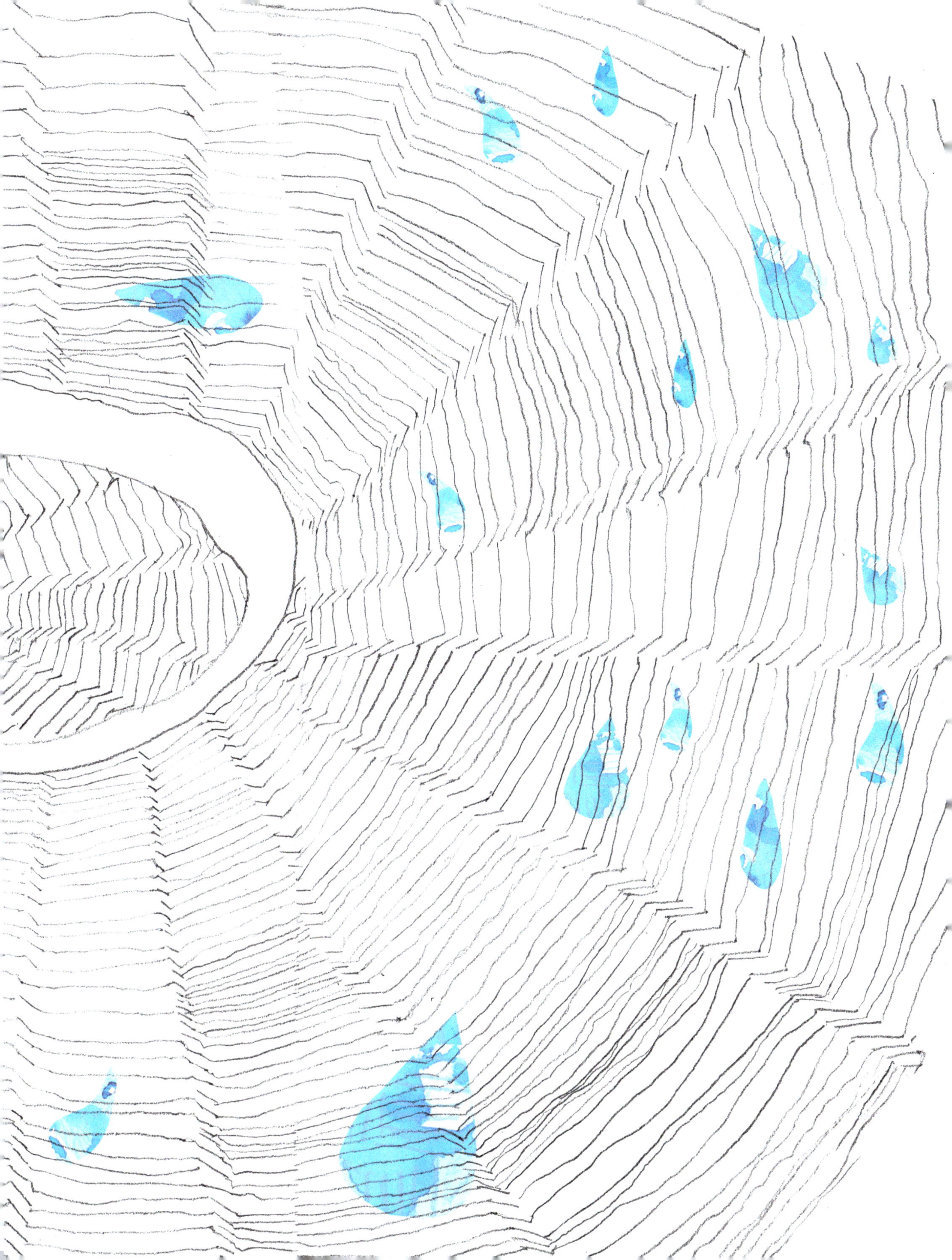

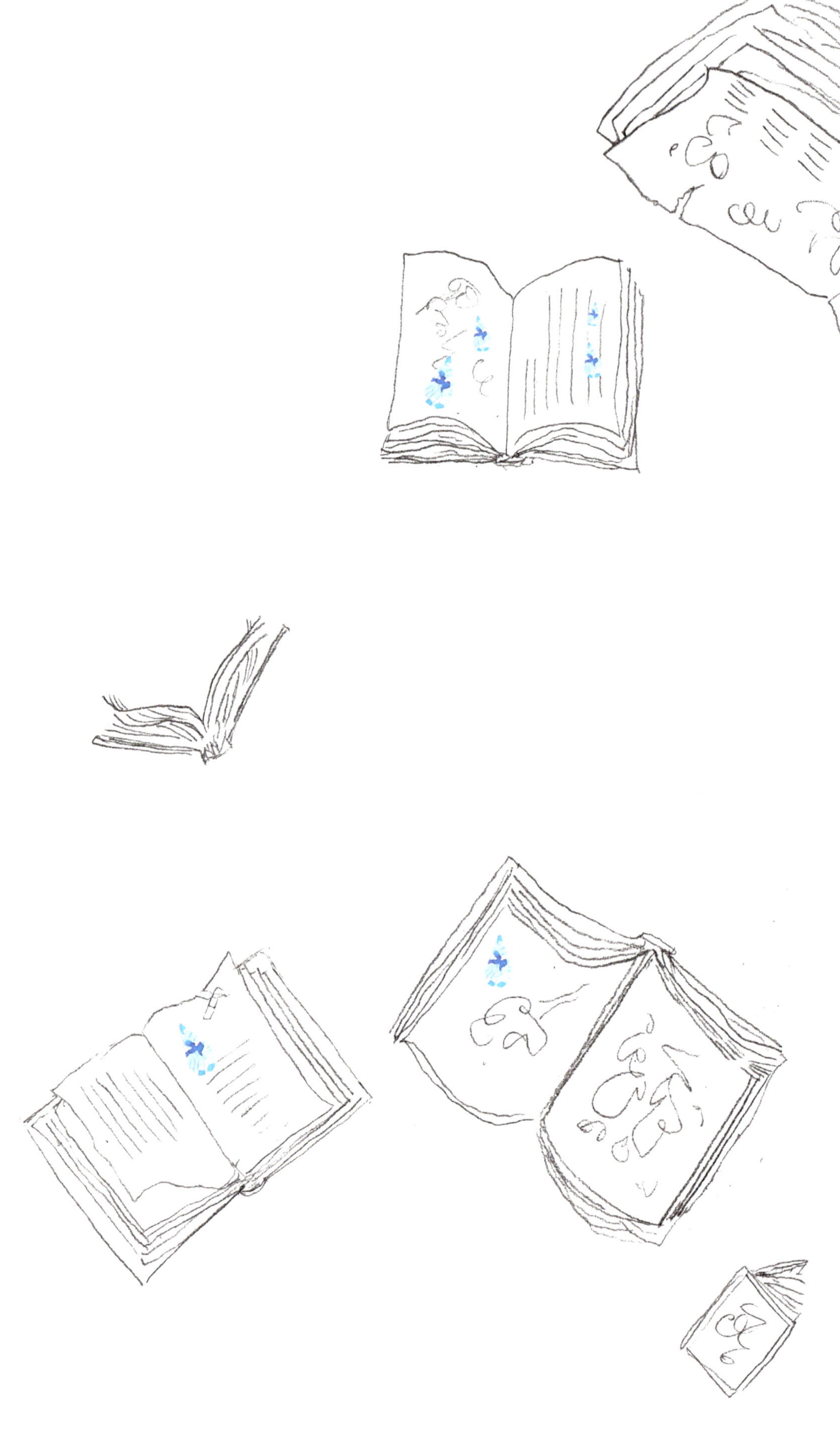

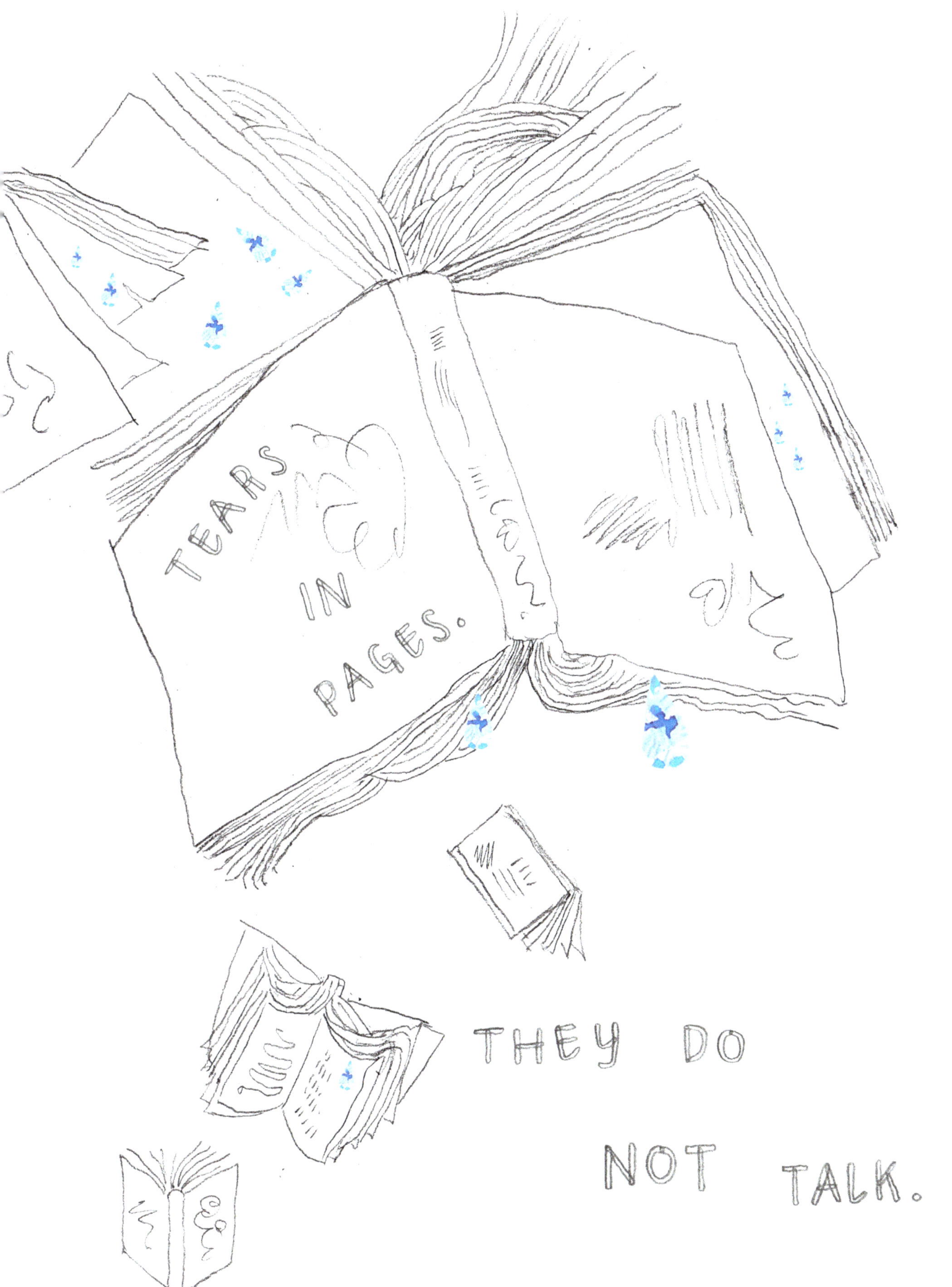

TEARS
IN
PAGES.
THEY DO
NOT TALK.

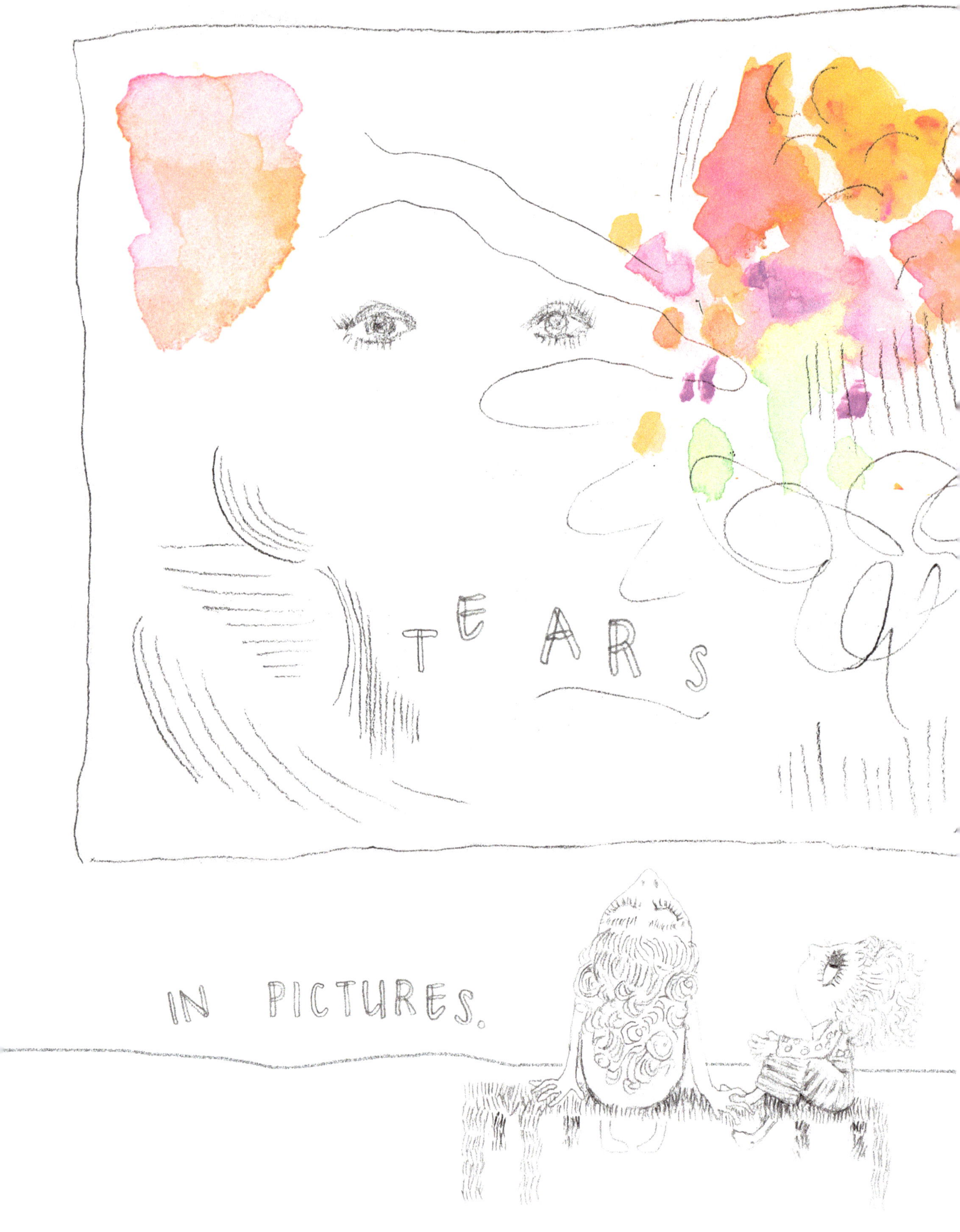

TEARS

IN PICTURES.

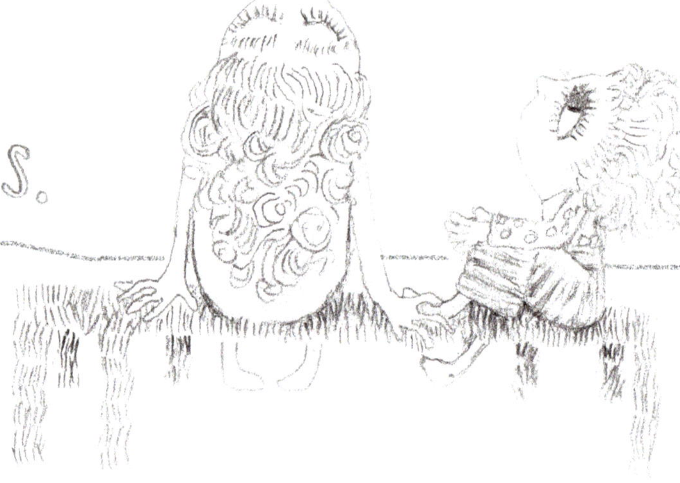

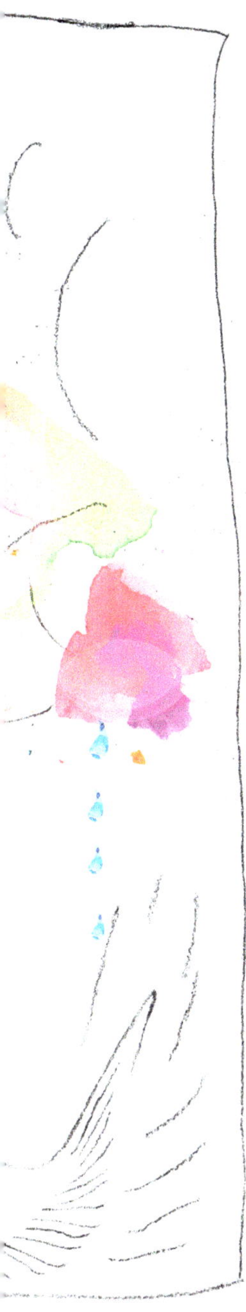
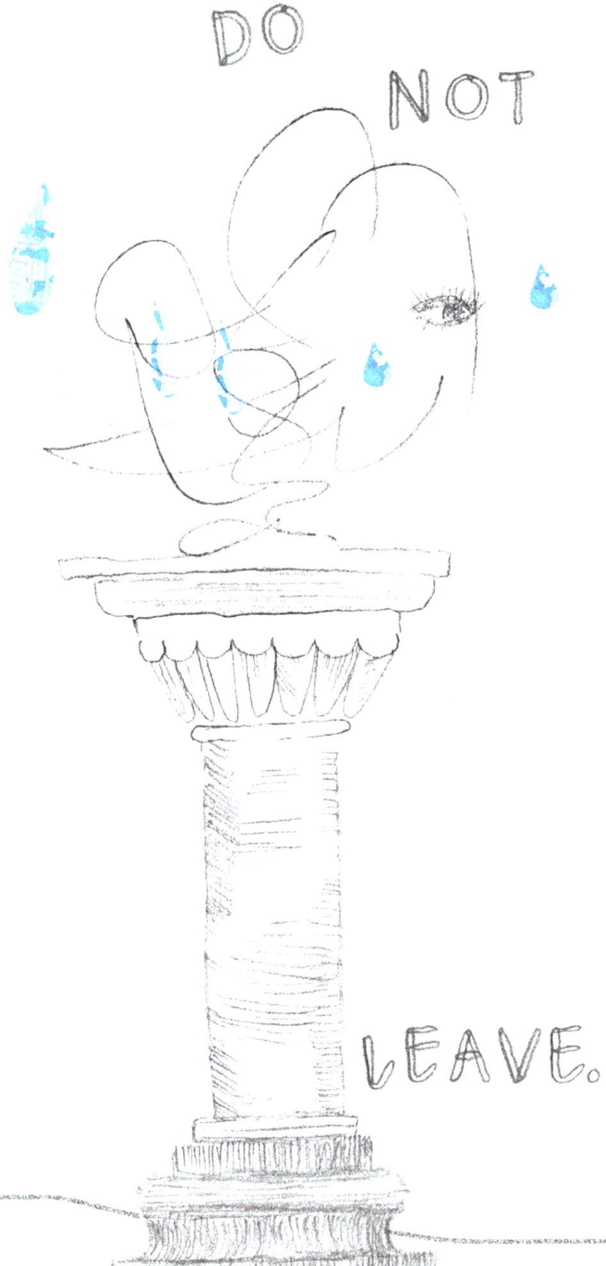
DO NOT
THEY
LEAVE.

LISTEN.

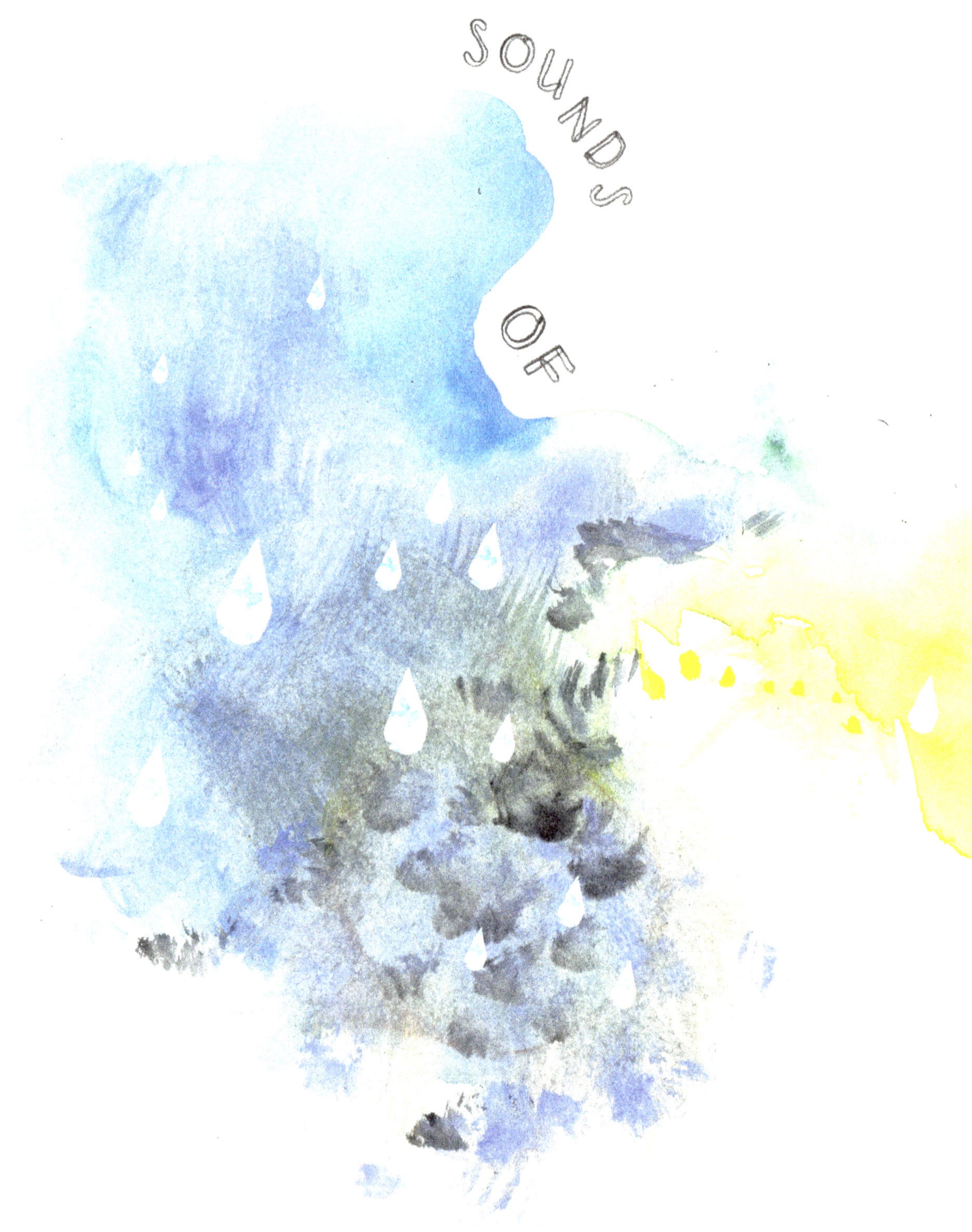

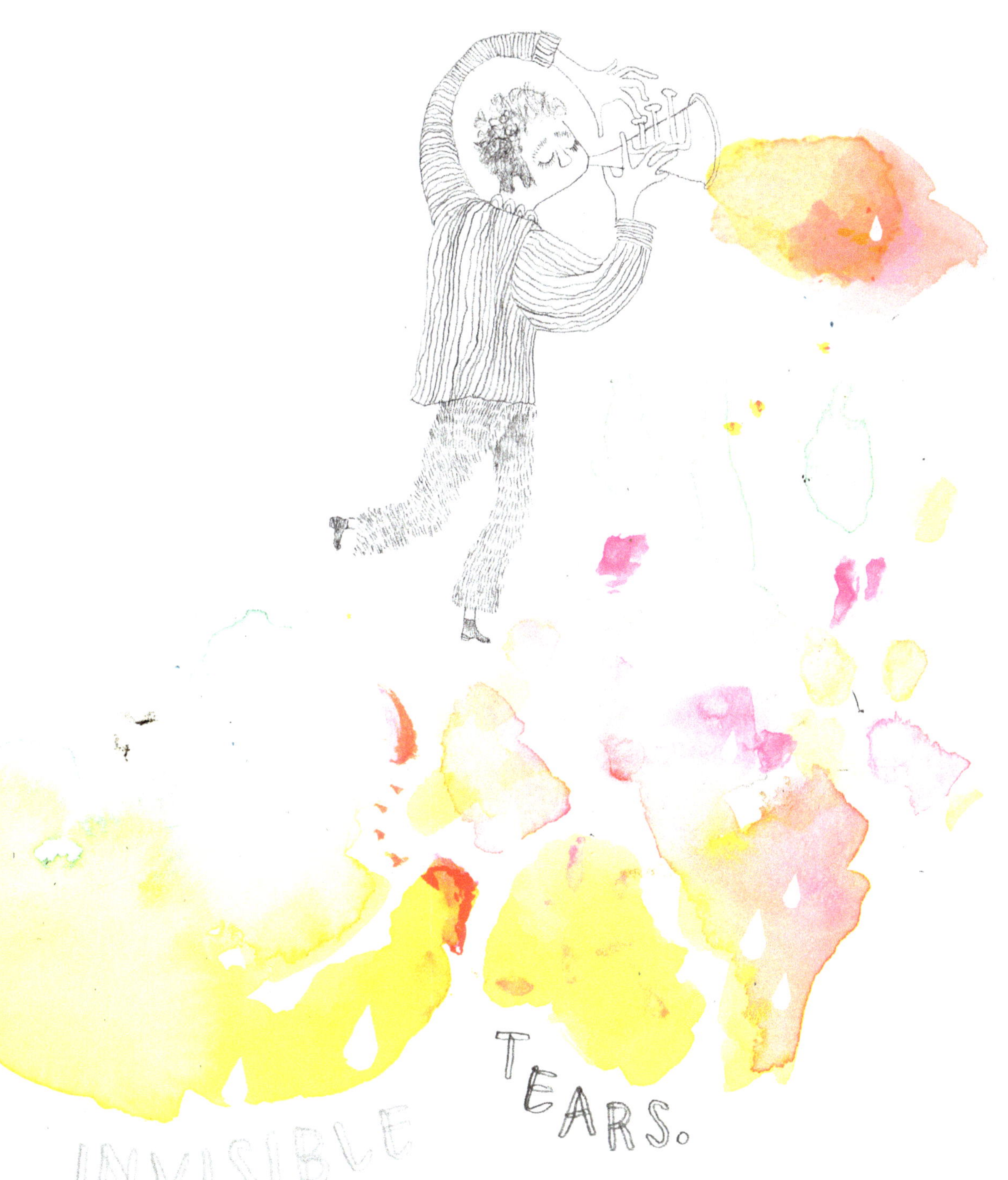

INVISIBLE TEARS.

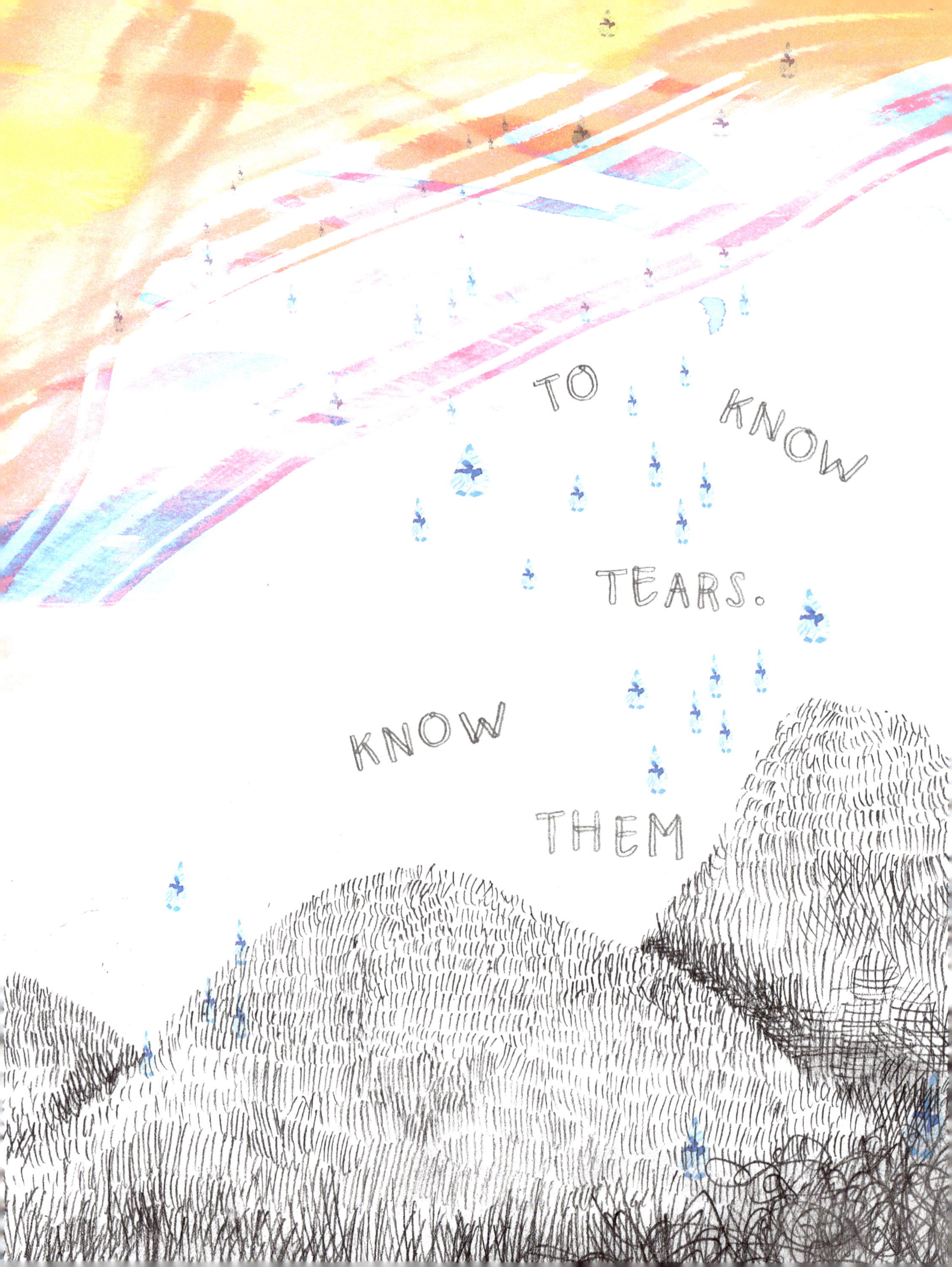

TO KNOW TEARS.
KNOW THEM

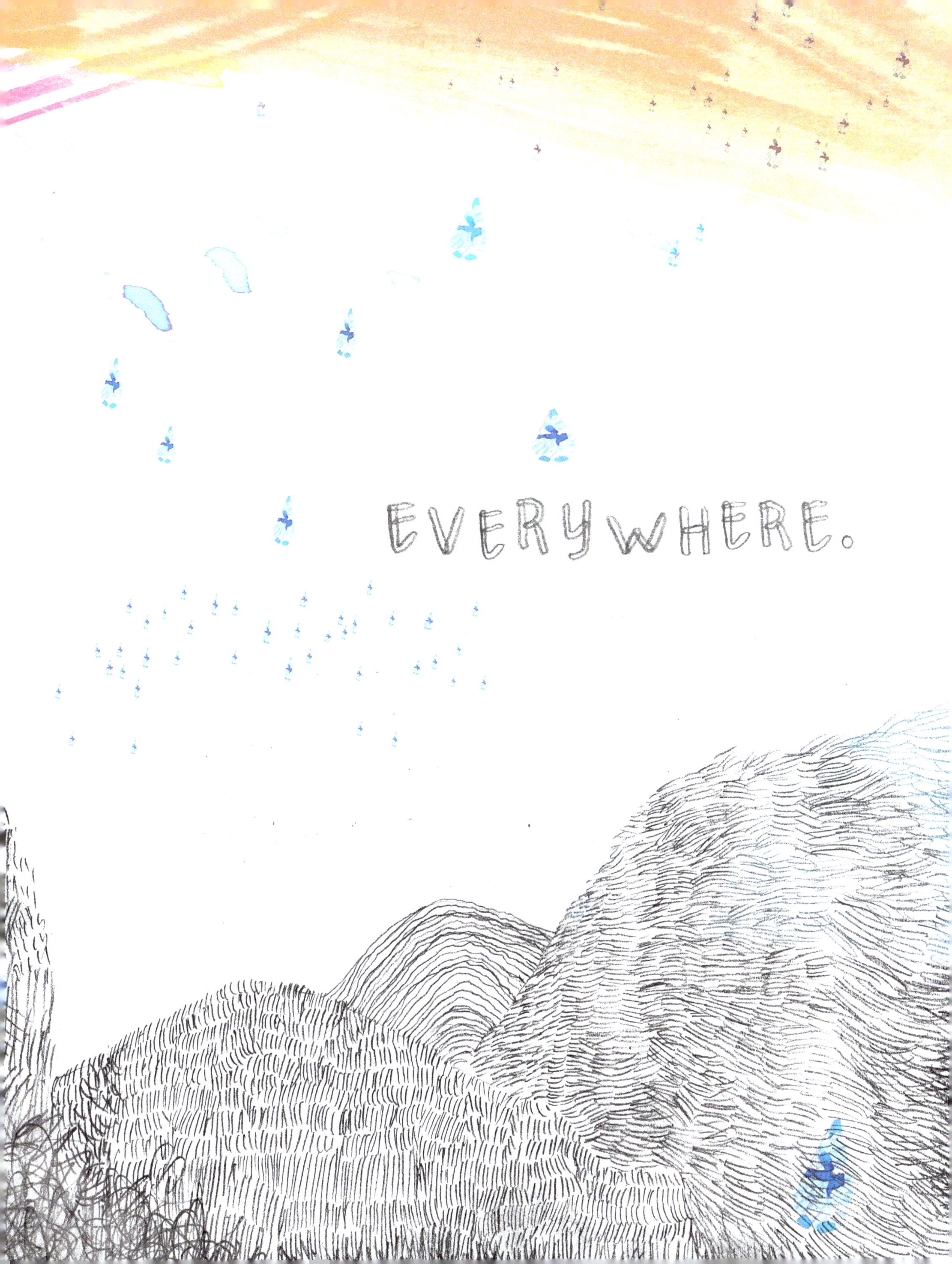

EVERYWHERE.

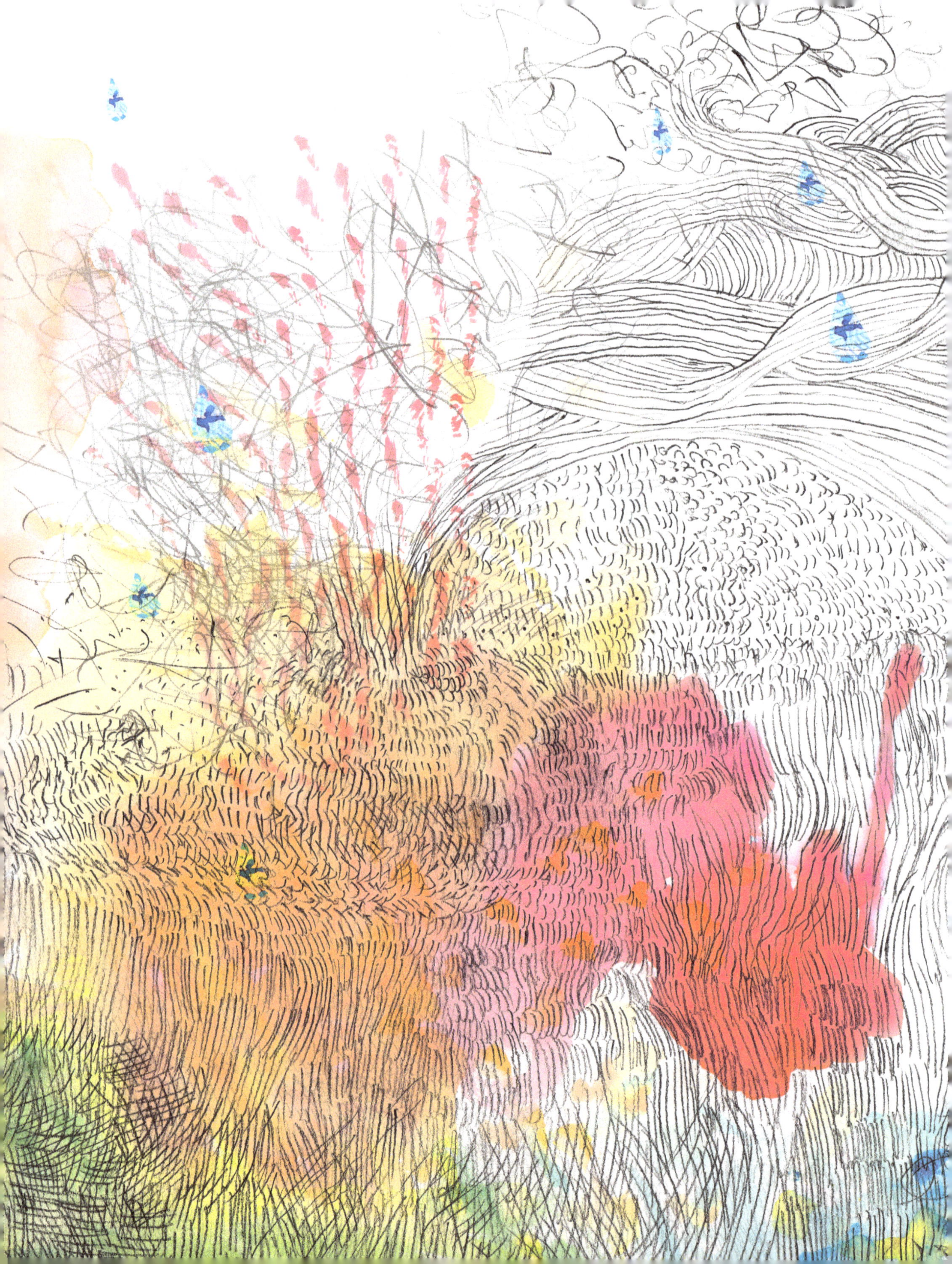

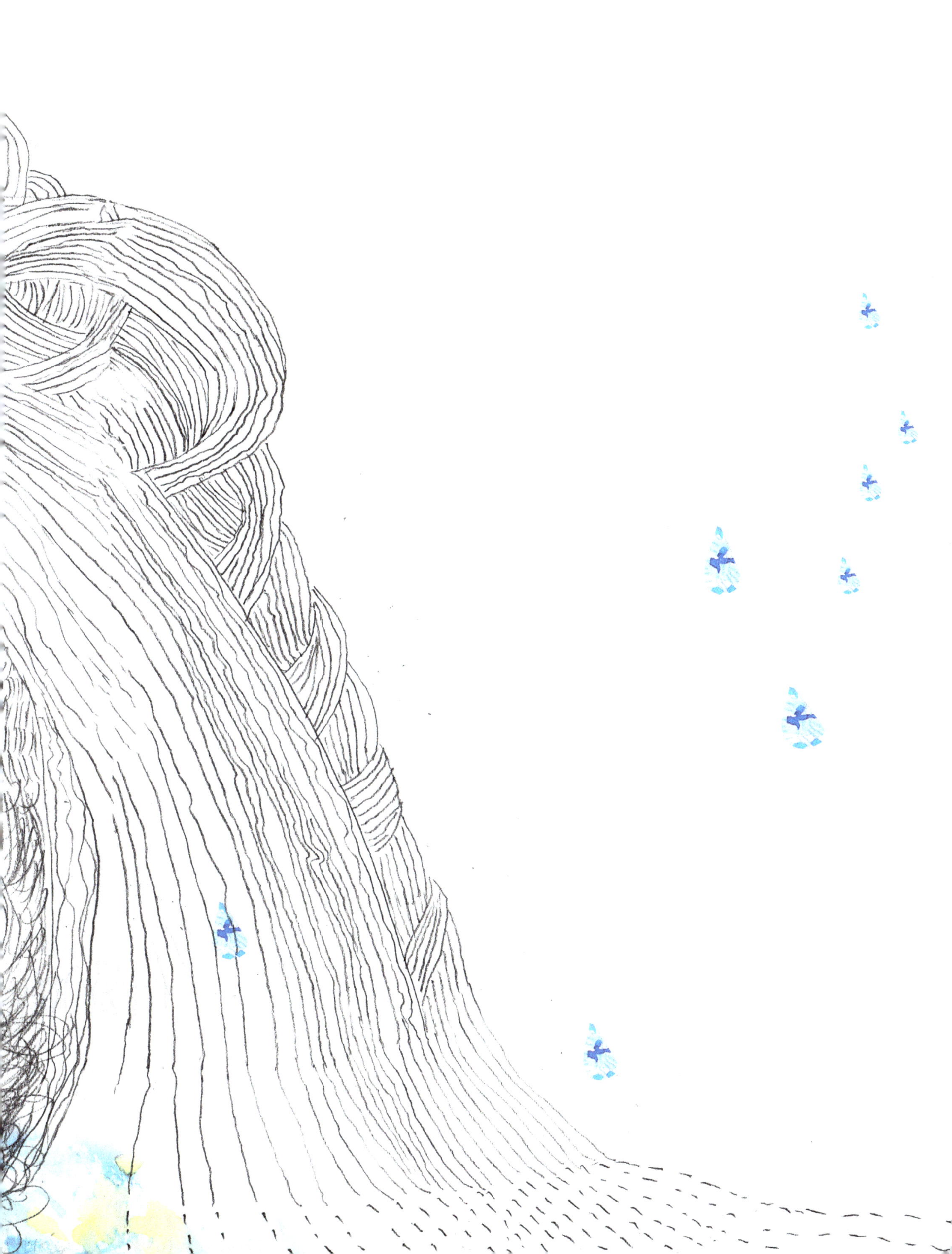

Kira Lynn Cain is an artist from California, USA.

She plays with drawing, words, and sometimes sound. Cain's sensibility is shaped by the idea of a dynamic interaction between a language and its audience. She earned her Bachelor of Fine Arts degree in New Genres from the San Francisco Art Institute. This is her first book.

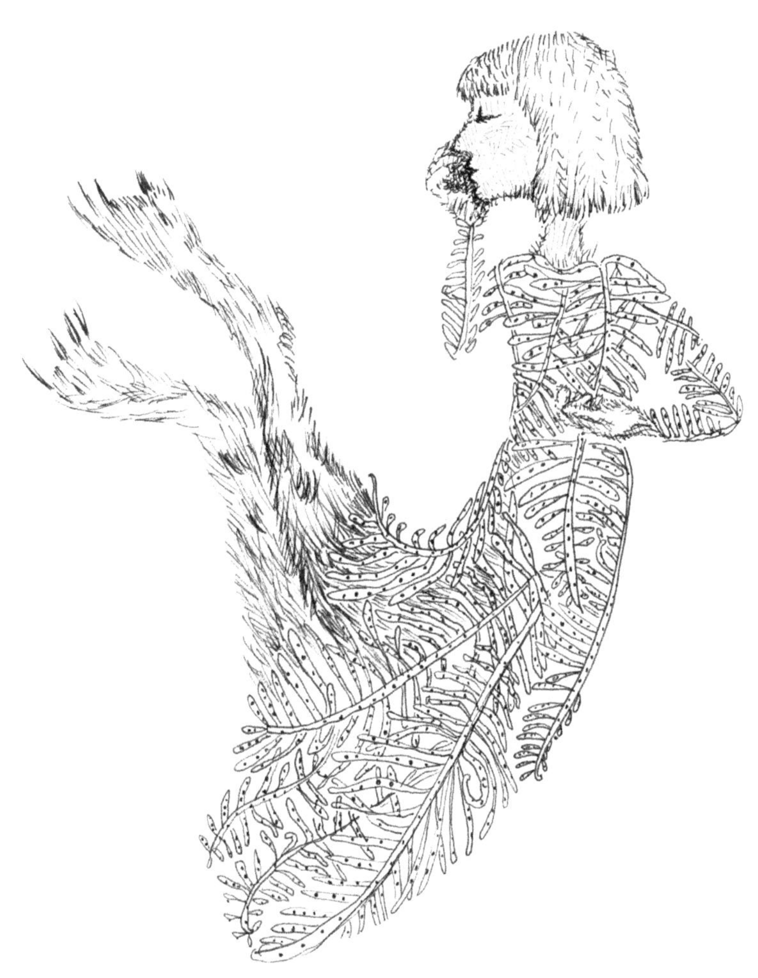